THE
WORDS
IN RED

THE TEACHINGS OF CHRIST COMPILED

Published by WORLD Bible Publishers
Iowa Falls, Iowa

THE WORDS IN RED

THE TEACHINGS OF CHRIST COMPILED

© Copyright 1989 by WORLD Bible Publishers

All Rights Reserved

Printed in the United States of America

Published by:

WORLD Bible Publishers
Iowa Falls, Iowa 50126

Compiled and Written By:
Michael Q. Pink

Cover Design By:
Mark Herron Productions

Book Design By:
Kerry Woo

ISBN 0-529-10009-6

Table of Contents

Introduction

We believe the whole bible to be the inspired Word of God. Yet the words of Jesus have special significance, as He came not to destroy the law, but to fulfill it.

The power of His words brought life to the dead, healing to the sick, hope to the hopeless and liberty to the oppressed. Still, the religious leadership of the day was caught up in man made traditions and steeped in hypocrisy.

The teachings of our Lord Jesus Christ, which changed the course of history are compiled topically to give you a fuller view and deeper understanding of the truths He left heaven to give to the world He would soon die for.

Study His teachings and let the Holy Spirit give you understanding; embrace His words and live.

Michael Q. Pink

Michael Q. Pink
Compiler

1. WHO JESUS IS

I am the Son of man[1], come to save that which was lost[2] and have power on earth to forgive sins.[3] I am the Son of God[4] your Master, even Christ,[5] the faithful and true witness,[6] the Alpha and Omega, the beginning and the end,[7] and the bright and morning star.[8]

I am the door of the sheep[9] and the good shepherd giving my life for the sheep.[10] By me if any man shall enter in, he shall be saved, and shall go in and out, and find pasture.[9] I have come from the Father[11] and as the Father has loved me, so I have loved you.[12] Take my yoke upon you and learn of me; for I am meek and lowly in heart: and you will find rest for your soul.[13]

I am in the Father, and the Father is in me[14] and if I do not the works of my Father, then do not believe me.[15] You call me Master and Lord, and you say well, for so I am,[16] and I am He that searches the heart and mind.[17]

I am the bread of life and he that comes to me will never hunger and he that believes on me shall never thirst.[18] Yes I am the living bread which came down from heaven: if any man eat of this bread, he will live forever: and the bread that I will give, is my flesh, which I will give for the life of the world.[19]

I am the light of the world and he that follows me will not walk in darkness, but will have the light of life.[20] I am the resurrection, and the life: he that believes in me, though he were dead, yet shall he live.[21] Yes, I am the way, the truth, and the life: no man comes to the Father, but by me.[22] I am holy and true, holding the Key of David; What I open, no man can shut and what I shut, no man can open.[23]

I am the true vine, my Father is the Gardener and you are the branches; Abide in me and be fruitful or abide not and wither.[24]

References:
1. Matthew 12:8
2. Matthew 18:11
3. Matthew 9:6
4. John 10:36
5. Matthew 23:10
6. Revelation 3:14
7. Revelation 22:13
8. Revelation 22:16
9. John 10:7 & 9
10. John 10:11
11. John 16:28
12. John 15:9
13. Matthew 11:29
14. John 14:11
15. John 10:37
16. John 13:13
17. Revelation 2:23
18. John 6:35
19. John 6:51
20. John 8:12
21. John 11:25
22. John 14:6
23. Revelation 3:7
24. John 15:1-6

2. HIS MISSION

I am come in my Fathers name,[1] from the Father to the world,[2] not to do my will, but the will of him that sent me. And this is the Fathers will, that everyone which sees the Son, and believes on Him, may have everlasting life: and I will raise him up at the last day.[3]

The Spirit of the Lord is upon me, because he has anointed me to preach the gospel to the poor; he has sent me to heal the broken hearted, to preach deliverance to the captives, and recovering of sight to the blind, to set at liberty them that are bruised, to preach the acceptable year of the Lord.[4] They that are whole have no need of the physician, but they that are sick: I came not to call the righteous, but sinners to repentance.[5] Yes the Son of man is come to seek and to save that which is lost.[6]

Think not that I came to destroy the law, or the prophets: I came not to destroy, but to fulfill.[7] I am come a light into the world, that whoever believes on me would not live in darkness.[8] The thief comes only to steal, kill and destroy; but I have come that you might have life, and have it more abundantly.[9]

I am the good shepherd[10] and I lay down my life for the sheep.[11] Therefore does my Father love me, because I lay down my life, that I may take it again.

No man takes it from me, but I lay it down of myself.[12] And I, if I be lifted up from the earth, will draw all men unto me.[13] When you have lifted up the Son of man then you will know that I am He, and that I do nothing of myself; but as my Father has taught me, I speak these things; for I do always those things that please him.[14] I must do the works of him that sent me, while it is day: the night is coming when no man can work.[15]

I came into this world to give sight to the spiritually blind and to show those who think they see, that they are really blind.[16] I proceeded forth and came from God, not of myself, but He sent me.[17] Think not, that I came to send peace on earth: I came not to send peace, but a sword[18] and division.[19] For I am come to set a man at variance against his father, and the daughter against her mother, and the daughter-in-law against her mother-in-law. And a mans foes will be they of his own household. He that loves father or mother more than me is not worthy of me: and he that loves son or daughter more than me is not worthy of me.[20]

Yes, the blind receive their sight, and the lame walk, the lepers are cleansed, and the deaf hear,[21] I cast out devils and do cures,[22] and the poor have the gospel preached to them;[21] For even the Son of man came not to be ministered to, but to minister.[23] I am among you as one who saves[24] and to give my life a ransom for many.[25]

You say I am a King. To this end was I born, and for this cause I came into the world, that I should bear witness to the truth. Every one that is of the truth, hears my voice.[26] And if any man hear my

4

words, and believe not, I judge him not: for I came not to judge the world, but to save the world. He that rejects me, and receives not my words, has one that judges him: the word that I have spoken, the same shall judge him in the last day.[27]

References:

1. John 5:43
2. John 16:28
3. John 6:38-40
4. Luke 4:18-19
5. Mark 2:17
6. Luke 19:10
7. Matthew 5:17
8. John 12:46
9. John 10:10
10. John 10:11
11. John 10:15
12. John 10:17-18
13. John 12:32
14. John 8:28-29
15. John 9:4
16. John 9:39
17. John 8:42
18. Matthew 10:34
19. Luke 12:51
20. Matthew 10:35-37
21. Matthew 11:5
22. Luke 13:32
23. Mark 10:45
24. Luke 22:27
25. Matthew 20:28
26. John 18:37
27. John 12:47-48

3. SALVATION AND ETERNAL LIFE

Truly, truly I tell you, Unless a man is born again, he cannot see the kingdom of God. Of a truth I tell you, Unless a man is born of water and of the Spirit, he cannot enter into the kingdom of God. That which is born of the flesh is flesh; and that which is born of the Spirit is spirit.

Marvel not that I told you, You must be born again. The wind blows where it wills, and you hear it, but cannot tell where it came from or where it is going: So is every one that is born of the Spirit. And as Moses lifted up the serpent in the wilderness, even so must the Son of man be lifted up: That whoever believes in him should not perish, but have eternal life. For God so loved the world, that He gave his only Son, that whoever believes in him should not perish, but have life everlasting. For God sent not his Son into the world to condemn the world; but that the world through him might be saved. He that believes on Him is not condemned: but he that believes not is condemned already, because he has not believed in the name of the only Son of God.[1]

And behold, one came and said to him, "Good Master, what good thing shall I do, that I may have eternal life?" And Jesus said to him, Why do you call me good? There is none good but one, that is

God: but if you will enter into life, keep the commandments. **And he answered, "Which?" Jesus said,** You shall not murder, You shall not commit adultery, You shall not steal, You shall not bear false witness, Honor your father and mother: and, You shall love your neighbor as yourself.

The young man said, "All these things have I kept from my youth up: what lack I yet?" Jesus said to him, If you will be perfect, go and sell what you have and give to the poor, and you will have treasure in heaven: and come and follow me. **But when the young man heard that saying, he went away sorrowful: for he had great possessions. Then Jesus said,** Truly I tell you, That a rich man shall hardly enter into the kingdom of heaven. It is easier for a camel to go through the eye of a needle, than for a rich man to enter into the kingdom of God. **When his disciples heard this, they were very amazed, saying, "Who then can be saved?" Jesus replied,** With men this is impossible; but with God all things are possible.[2]

A certain man had two sons: And the younger son gathered all together, and took his journey into a far country, and there wasted his money with riotous living. And when he had spent all, there arose a mighty famine in that land and he began to be in need. So he went to work for a local citizen who sent him into the fields to feed the pigs. He became so hungry that even the pigs food looked good to him, but no one fed him.

When he came to his senses, he realized that his fathers hired servants have more than enough food to eat and he was about to perish from starvation! So he decided to go back to his father

7

as one of his hired servants for he thought he was no more worthy to be called a son.

When he got near his fathers house, his father saw him and had compassion and ran and hugged and kissed him. And the son said, Father I have sinned against heaven and in your sight, and am no more worthy to be called your son. But the Father said to his servants, Bring out the best robe, and put it on him; and put a ring on his hand, and shoes on his feet: And bring the fatted calf, and kill it; and let us eat, and be merry: For this my son was dead, and is alive again; he was lost, and is found.

Now when his eldest son learned what had happened, he was angry, and would not join the party: So his father came out to him and pleaded with him to come in and join them. His son said, All these years I have served you, never disobeying and yet you never had a party like this for me: But when my brother gets home after wasting your money on harlots, you kill the fatted calf for him.

And the Father said, Son, you are always with me, and all that I have is yours but it is fitting that we should celebrate, and be glad: for your brother was dead, and is alive again; and was lost, and is found.[3]

What man of you, having a hundred sheep, if he lose one of them, does not leave the ninety-nine in the wilderness, and go after that which is lost, until he finds it? And when he has found it, lays it on his shoulders, rejoicing. And when he comes home, he calls together his friends and neighbors, saying, Rejoice with me; for I have found my sheep which was lost. I say to you, that likewise joy shall be in heaven over one sinner that repents, more than over ninety-nine just persons, which need no repentance.[4]

Truly I say, He that hears my word, and believes on him that sent me, has everlasting life, and shall not come into condemnation; but is passed from death to life.[5] No man can come to me, except the Father which sent me, draw him: and I will raise him up at the last day.[6] He that believes on me has life everlasting.[7]

Whoever will confess me before men, him will I confess also before my Father which is in heaven. But whoever denies me before men, him will I also deny before my Father.[8] For whoever is ashamed of me and of my words, of him shall the Son of man be ashamed, when he comes in his own glory, and in his Father's, and of the holy angels.[9]

And Jesus said to the Father, This is life eternal, that they might know thee the only true God, and Jesus Christ, who you have sent.[10]

References:
1. *John 3:3-18*
2. *Matthew 19:16-26*
3. *Luke 15:11-32*
4. *Luke 15:4-7*
5. *John 5:24*
6. *John 6:44*
7. *John 6:47*
8. *Matthew 10:32-33*
9. *Luke 9:26*
10. *John 17:1 & 3*

4. OUR RELATIONSHIP WITH JESUS AND THE FATHER

Behold, I stand at the door, and knock: if any man hear my voice, and open the door, I will come in to him, and will sup with him and he with me.[1] No longer do I call you servants; for the servant knows not what his Lord does: but I have called you friends; for I have made known to you all things that I heard of my Father.[2] Greater love has no man than this, that a man lay down his life for his friends; and you are my friends, if you do whatever I command you.[3]

You have not chosen me, but I have chosen you, and ordained you, that you should go and bring forth fruit, and that your fruit should remain: that whatever you ask of the Father in my name, he may give it you.[4] Yes, I am the true vine, and my Father is the Gardener. Every branch in me that does not bear fruit, he takes away and every branch that bears fruit, he prunes, that it may bring forth more fruit. Abide in me, and I in you. As the branch cannot bear fruit of itself, unless it abides in the vine, neither will you, unless you abide in me: for without me you can do nothing.[5]

I am in you, and the Father is in me, that you may

be made perfect in one and that the world may know that He sent me, and loves you as He loves me.[6] Yes, as the Father has loved me, so I have loved you: continue in my love. If you keep my commandments, you will abide in my love; even as I have kept my Fathers commandments, and abide in His love.[7]

He that has my commandments, and keeps them is he that loves me.[8] In fact, if you love me, keep my commandments.[9] He that loves me shall be loved of my Father, and I will love him, and reveal myself to him.[8] Yes, if a man loves me, he will keep my words and my Father will love him, and we will come unto him, and make our abode with him.[10]

I will pray to the Father, and He will give you another Comforter, that he may live with you forever-the Spirit of Truth; whom the world cannot receive, because it neither sees him or knows him: but you know him; for he dwells with you, and will be in you.[11] For the hour comes, and now is, when the true worshippers will worship the Father in Spirit and in truth: for the Father seeks such to worship Him.[12]

No man can come to me, except the Father which sent me draw him: and I will raise him up at the last day.[13] And all that the Father gives me, will come to me; and he that comes to me, I will not at all cast out.[14] And whoever, does the will of my Father which is in heaven, the same is my brother, and sister, and mother.[15]

My sheep hear my voice, and I know them, and they follow me: And I give them eternal life; and they will never perish, neither will any man pluck them out of my hand. My Father, which gave them to me, is greater than all; and no man is able to pluck them out of my Father's hand.[16]

References:

1. Revelations 3:20
2. John 15:15
3. John 15:13-14
4. John 15:16
5. John 15:1-5
6. John 17:23
7. John 15:9-10
8. John 14:21
9. John 14:15
10. John 14:23
11. John 14:16-17
12. John 4:23
13. John 6:44
14. John 6:37
15. Matthew 12:50
16. John 10:27-29

5. THE KINGDOM OF GOD

Happy and blessed are the poor in spirit[1] and those who are persecuted because of righteousness: for theirs is the kingdom of heaven.[2] But unless you are converted and become as little children, you will not enter into the kingdom of heaven.[3] Truly, I tell you, unless a man is born again, he cannot see the kingdom of God.[4] Yes, except a man be born of water and of the Spirit, he cannot enter into the kingdom of God. That which is born of the flesh is flesh; and that which is born of the Spirit is spirit.[5]

The law and the prophets were until John: since then the kingdom of God is preached[6] and is advancing forcefully. Men of violence take it by force[7] and every one is pressing into it.[6] It's like a treasure, hidden in a field, which when a man found it, he hid it, and with great joy went and sold all that he had, and bought the field.[8] Or like a merchant man, seeking beautiful pearls, who, when he had found one pearl of great price, went and sold all that he had, and bought it.[9]

This kingdom does not come with observation, neither shall they say, it's here! or it's there! For behold, the kingdom of God is within you[10] And whoever will not receive the kingdom of God as a little child will in no way enter in,[11] for of such is the kingdom of heaven.[12] Whoever therefore will humble himself as a little child, the same is greatest in the kingdom of heaven.[13]   But unless your righteousness exceeds that of the scribes and Pharisees, you will in no case enter into the kingdom of heaven.[14]   Not every one that says to me, Lord, Lord, will enter into the kingdom of heaven; but he that does the will of my Father which is in heaven.[15]

What do you think? A certain man had two sons; and he came to the first, and said, Son, go work today in my vineyard.   And he answered, I will not: but later repented and went.   And he came to the second son, and said the same.   And he answered, I will go, but he didn't.   Which of the two did his father's will? The first son. Truly, I tell you, that the tax collectors and prostitutes will enter the kingdom of God before you Pharisees, for they believe the way of righteousness preached by John and you didn't.[16]

Listen, there went out a sower to sow,[17] and when he sowed, some seeds fell by the wayside;[18] and were trampled on, and the fowls of the air devoured them.[19]   And some fell on stony ground, where it had only a little earth; and immediately it sprang up, because it had only a little earth: But when the sun was up, it was scorched; and because it had no root,[17] and lacked moisture, it withered away.[19] And some fell among thorns, and the thorns grew up, and choked it, and it yielded no fruit.   And other fell on good ground, and did yield fruit that sprang up and increased; and brought forth some thirty, and some sixty, and some one hundredfold increase.   He that has ears to hear, let him hear.[17]

Do you not understand this parable? How then

will you know all parables?[20] Now the parable is this: the seed is the Word of God. Those by the way side are they that hear,[22] but don't understand it, then comes the wicked one, Satan, and takes away the word that was sown in their heart,[21] lest they should believe and be saved.[22] And these are they which are sown on stony ground; who, when they have heard the word, immediately receive it with gladness[20] and joy.[22] Yet, he has no root in himself[21] and believes for a while,[22] then later, when affliction,[20] tribulation[21] or persecution arises for the words sake, immediately they are offended,[20] and in time of temptation fall away.[22] And these are they which are sown among thorns[20] which, when they have heard the word, go forth[22] and the cares of this world, the deceitfulness of riches[20] and pleasures,[22] and the lusts of other things entering in, choke the word,[20] and he becomes unfruitful,[21] and brings no fruit to perfection.[22]

But he that received the seed into the good ground is he that hears the word, and understands it,[21] which in an honest and good heart, having heard the word[22] and received it,[20] keeps it and brings forth fruit with patience[22] some thirtyfold, some sixty, and some one hundredfold.[20]

So, the kingdom of God, is like a man who casts seed into the ground, then sleeps, rising night and day, and the seed begins to spring and grow up, though he doesn't know how. For the earth brings forth fruit of herself; first the blade, then the ear, after that the full corn in the ear. But when the fruit is brought forth, immediately he puts the sickle to it, because the harvest has come.[23]

What is the kingdom of God like? What does it resemble?[24] or with what can we compare it?[25] The kingdom of heaven is similar to a grain of mustard seed, which a man took and sowed in his field, which indeed is the smallest of all seeds:[26] But when it is sown, it grows up, and becomes the greatest of all herbs, and shoots out great branches; so that the fowls of the air may lodge under the shadow of it.[25] Likewise, the kingdom of heaven is like leaven, which a woman took, and hid in three measures of meal, until it was all leavened.[27]

Fear not, little flock; for it is your Father's good pleasure to give you the kingdom,[28] but no man, having put his hand to the plough, and looking back is fit for the kingdom of God.[29] And I say unto you, Among those that are born of women, there is not a greater prophet than John the Baptist: but he that is least in the kingdom of God is greater than he.[30] And every teacher of the law which is instructed about the kingdom of heaven is like a man that is a householder, which brings forth out of his treasure things both new and old.[31]

Take no thought saying, "What will we eat?" or "What will we drink?" or " What will we wear?" (For after all these things do the Gentiles seek:) for your heavenly Father knows that you need all these things. Seek the kingdom of God first, and his righteousness; and all these things will be added to you.[32] Children, how hard it is for them that trust in riches to enter the kingdom of God![33] There is no man that has left house, or parents, or brothers,[34] or sister,[35] or wife, or children,[34] or lands,[35] for the sake of the kingdom of God,[34] who

16

won't receive a hundredfold now in this time, houses, brothers, sisters, mothers, children and lands with persecutions; and in the world to come eternal life. But many that are first shall be last; and the last first.[36]

The kingdom of God is like a net that was cast into the sea, and gathered of every kind. When it was full, they went to shore, sat down, and gathered the good into vessels, but threw the bad away. So will it be at the end of the world: the angels will come forth, and sever the wicked from among the just, and throw them into the furnace of fire: there will be wailing and gnashing of teeth.[37]

Again, the kingdom of heaven is like a man who sowed good seed in his field. But while men slept, his enemy came and sowed tares among the wheat, and went his way. And when the blade was sprung up, and brought forth fruit, then the tares also appeared. So the servants of the householder came to him and said, Did you not sow good seed in your field? where did the tares come from? He replied, An enemy has done this. The servants said, Should we go and gather them up? But he said, No; lest while you gather up the tares, you uproot the wheat with them. Let both grow together until the harvest: and in the time of harvest I will say to the reapers, Gather first the tares, and bind them in bundles to burn them: but gather the wheat into my barn.[38]

Now he that sows the good seed is the Son of man; The field is the world; the good seed are the children of the kingdom; but the tares are the children of the wicked one. The enemy that sowed them is the devil; the harvest is the end of the world; and the reapers are the angels. Therefore as the tares are gathered and burned in the fire; so shall it be in the end of this world. The Son of man will send forth his angels, and they will gather out of his kingdom, all things that offend, and those who do iniquity; And shall throw them into a furnace of fire: there will be wailing and gnashing of teeth. Then the righteous will shine as the sun in the kingdom of their Father. Whoever has ears to hear, let him hear.[39]

Then shall the kingdom of heaven be compared to ten virgins, which took their lamps, and went forth to meet the bridegroom. And five of them were wise, and five were foolish. They that were foolish took their lamps, and took no oil with them:[40] But the wise took oil in their vessels with their lamps. While the bridegroom tarried, they all slumbered and slept. And at midnight there was a cry made, Behold, the bridegroom comes; go out to meet him. Then all those virgins arose, and trimmed their lamps. And the foolish said unto the wise, Give us of your oil; for our lamps are gone out. But the wise answered, saying, Not so; lest there be not enough for us and you: but go rather to them that sell, and buy for yourselves. And while they went to buy, the bridegroom came; and they that were ready went in with him to the marriage: and the door was shut. Afterward came also the other virgins, saying Lord, Lord, open to us. But he answered and said, Verily I say unto you, I know you not.[41] And I say unto you, That many shall come from the east and west, and shall sit down with Abraham, and Isaac, and Jacob, in the kingdom of heaven. But the children of the kingdom shall be cast out into outer darkness: there shall be weeping and gnashing of teeth.[42]

And I will give to you the keys of the kingdom of heaven: and whatever you bind on earth, will be bound in heaven: and whatever you loose on earth will be loosed in heaven.[43] And this gospel of the kingdom, will be preached in all the world for a witness to all nations and then will the end come.[44]

References:

1. *Matthew 5:3*
2. *Matthew 5:10*
3. *Matthew 18:3*
4. *John 3:3*
5. *John 3:5-6*
6. *Luke 16:16*
7. *Matthew 11:12*
8. *Matthew 13:44*
9. *Matthew 13:45-46*
10. *Luke 17:20-21*
11. *Luke 18:17*
12. *Matthew 19:14*
13. *Matthew 18:4*
14. *Matthew 5:20*
15. *Matthew 7:21*
16. *Matthew 21:28-32*
17. *Mark 4:3-9*
18. *Matthew 13:3-9*
19. *Luke 8:5-8*
20. *Mark 4:13-20*
21. *Matthew 13:12-23*
22. *Luke 8:11-15*
23. *Mark 4:26-29*
24. *Luke 13:19*
25. *Mark 4:30-32*
26. *Matthew 13:31*
27. *Matthew 13:33*
28. *Luke 12:32*
29. *Luke 9:62*
30. *Luke 7:28*
31. *Matthew 13:52*
32. *Matthew 6:31-33*
33. *Mark 10:24*
34. *Luke 18:29*
35. *Matthew 19:29*
36. *Mark 10:30-31*
37. *Matthew 13:47-50*
38. *Matthew 13:24-30*
39. *Matthew 13:36-43*
40. *Matthew 25:1-3*
41. *Matthew 25:4-12*
42. *Matthew 8:11-12*
43. *Matthew 16:19*
44. *Matthew 24:14*

6. SATAN'S KINGDOM

Every kingdom divided against itself is brought to desolation; and every city or house divided against itself will not stand.[1] If Satan is divided against himself, how can his kingdom stand?[2] If Satan cast out Satan, he is divided against himself[3] and cannot stand but has an end.[4]

And if I by Satan, cast out devils, by whom do your children cast them out? Let them be your judges. But if I with the finger of God cast out devils by[5] the Spirit of God, then the kingdom of God is come upon you.[6] When a strong man that is armed, keeps his palace, his goods are in peace. But when a stronger than he comes upon him, and overcomes him, he takes from him all his armor which he trusted in, and divides his spoil.[7] But no man can enter into a strong man's house, and take his goods, unless he first bind the strong man; then he will take of his goods.[8]

He that is not with me is against me; and he that gathers not with me, scatters everywhere.[9] When the unclean spirit is gone out of a man, he walks through dry places, seeking rest, and finds none. Then he says, I will return into my house from where I came out; and when he is come, he finds it empty, swept, and garnished. Then he goes, and takes with himself seven other spirits more wicked than himself, and they enter in and dwell there:

20

and the last state of that man is worse than the first.[10]

It is the devil that catches the word out of the hearts of men, when they don't understand it,[11] lest they should believe and be saved.[12] Satan savors not the things that be of God.[13] He was a murderer from the beginning, not holding to the truth, because there is no truth in him. When he speaks a lie, he speaks his language: for he is a liar, and the father of it.[14] He is a thief, coming only to steal, kill and destroy,[15] but now is the judgement of this world: now shall the prince of this world be cast out,[16] because the prince of this world is judged.[17]

And I beheld Satan fall from heaven like lightning. Behold I give you power and authority to tread on serpents and scorpions, and over all the power of the enemy: and nothing shall by any means hurt you. Nevertheless, do not rejoice in this, rather rejoice that your names are written in heaven.[18]

References:
1. Matthew 12:25
2. Luke 11:18
3. Matthew 12:26
4. Mark 3:26
5. Luke 11:19-20
6. Matthew 12:28
7. Luke 11:21-22
8. Mark 3:27
9. Luke 11:23
10. Matthew 12:43-45
11. Matthew 13:19
12. Luke 8:12
13. Mark 8:33
14. John 8:44
15. John 10:10
16. John 12:31
17. John 16:11
18. Luke 10:18-20

7. PRAYER

Men ought always to pray, and not to faint,[1] so watch therefore, and pray always that you may be counted worthy to escape all these things that shall come to pass, and to stand before the Son of man.[2] Yes, pray for them which despitefully use you, and persecute you[3] and pray also that the Lord of the harvest would send forth laborers into his harvest.[4]

Take heed, watch and pray: for you know not when the time is.[5] Yes, watch and pray lest you enter into temptation, for the spirit truly is ready, but the flesh is weak.[6] And when you pray, do not be like the hypocrites, for they love to pray standing in the synagogues and in the corners of the streets, that they may be seen by men. Truly, they have their reward.[7]

But when you pray, go in your closet, and when you have shut the door, pray to your Father in secret; and your Father which sees in secret, will reward you openly. But when you pray, don't use vain repetitions, as the heathen do: for they think they will be heard for their much speaking. Therefore, don't be like them; for your Father knows what things you have need of, before you ask him.[8]

Pray in this way: Our Father which is in heaven, hallowed be your name. Your kingdom come. Your will be done in earth as it is in heaven. Give us this day our daily bread. And forgive us our debts, as we forgive our debtors. And lead us not into temptation, but deliver us from evil. For thine is the kingdom, and the power, and the glory, for ever. Amen.[9]

When you pray, forgive anyone you have ought against[10] or who has trespassed against you, so your heavenly Father will also forgive you: But if you do not forgive men their trespasses, neither will your heavenly Father forgive your trespasses.[11]

Which of you, who has a friend will go to him at midnight and say, "Friend, lend me three loaves; for a friend of mine on a journey has come to me and I have nothing to set before him." Then he answers from within, "Don't trouble me: my door is shut, and my children are with me in bed; I cannot rise and give you anything." I tell you, though he will not rise and give him because he is his friend, yet because of his shameless persistence he will rise and give him all he needs.[12]

I say to you, ask and it shall be given to you; seek and you will find; knock and it will be opened to you. For every one that asks, receives; and he that seeks, finds; and to him that knocks it shall be opened.[13] Whatever you ask in my name, that will I do, that the Father may be glorified in the Son. If you ask anything in my name, I will do it.[14] Before now, you asked nothing in my name: ask, and you will receive, that your joy may be full.[15]

Prayer Habits of Jesus
1) And in the morning, rising up a great while before day, he went out, and departed into a solitary place, and there prayed.[16]

2) And when he had sent them away, he departed into a mountain to pray.[17]
3) And he withdrew himself into the wilderness, and prayed.[18]
4) And when he had sent the multitudes away, he went up into a mountain apart to pray: and when the evening was come, he was there alone.[19]
5) And it came to pass in those days, that he went out into a mountain to pray, and continued all night in prayer to God.[20]

Truly, I tell you, Whatever you bind on earth will be bound in heaven: and whatever you loose on earth will be loosed in heaven. Again I tell you, That if two of you shall agree on earth as touching anything that they shall ask, it will be done for them, of my Father which is in heaven. For where two or three are gathered together in my name, there am I in the midst of them.[21]

But seek not what you will eat or drink, neither be of a doubtful mind. For all these things do the nations of the world seek after: and your Father knows that you have need of these things. But rather, seek the kingdom of God and all these things will be added to you.[22]

Two men went up into the temple to pray; the one a Pharisee, and the other a publican. The Pharisee stood and prayed saying, God, I thank you, that I am not as other men are, extortioners, unjust, adulterers, or even as this publican. I fast twice in the week, I give tithes of all that I possess. And the publican, standing afar off, would not lift up so much as his eyes unto heaven, but beat upon his breast, saying, God be merciful to me a sinner. I tell you, this man went down to his house justified rather than the other: for every one that exalts himself will be abased; and he that humbles himself will be exalted.[23]

And the hour is coming, and now is, when the true worshippers will worship the Father in spirit and in truth: for the Father seeks such to worship him. God is a Spirit: and they that worship him must worship him in spirit and in truth.[24] Remember, whatever you ask in prayer, believing, you will receive.[25]

References:

1. Luke 18:1
2. Luke 21:36
3. Matthew 5:44
4. Luke 10:2
5. Mark 13:33
6. Mark 14:38
7. Matthew 6:5
8. Matthew 6:6-8
9. Matthew 6:9-13
10. Mark 11:25
11. Matthew 6:14-15
12. Luke 11:5-8
13. Luke 11:9-10
14. John 14:13-14
15. John 16:24
16. Mark 1:35
17. Mark 6:46
18. Luke 5:16
19. Matthew 14:23
20. Luke 6:12
21. Matthew 18:18-20
22. Luke 12:29-31
23. Luke 18:10-14
24. John 4:23-24
25. Matthew 21:22

8. FIRST THINGS FIRST

1) Seek first the kingdom of God, and his righteousness and all your needs will be provided.[1]

2) If your brother has something against you, first make reconciliation with him then offer your gift at the alter.[2]

3) Before correcting your brothers minor faults, which are as specks in his eye, First correct your faults, which are like logs in your own eye! Then you will see clearly to take the speck from your brother's eye.[3, 4]

4) Before plundering Satan's kingdom, he must first be bound, then his demons can be cast out.[5,6]

5) Love the Lord your God with all your heart, and with all your soul and with all your mind,[7] and with all your strength, This is the first[8] and great commandment.[7]

6) Hypocrites, clean the outside of the cup, but are full of greed, extortion[9] and wickedness[10] on the inside. You must first, clean the inside of the cup, and then the whole cup will be clean.[9] Give of the things you have and all things will be clean for you.[10]

7) The earth brings forth fruit of herself; first the

blade, then the ear, after that, the full corn in the ear.[11]

8) When you enter a house, first say, "Peace be to this house". And if a man of peace is there, your peace will rest on him, but if not, it will return to you.[12]

9) Before you build a tower, first count the cost, to determine if you have sufficient to finish it.[13]

10) Before a king wages war with another king, he first should assess how the number of his troops he has will fare against the number of troops the opposing king has.[14]

References:
1. Matthew 6:33
2. Matthew 5:23-24
3. Matthew 7:3-5
4. Luke 6:41-42
5. Matthew 12:29
6. Mark 3:27
7. Matthew 22:37
8. Mark 12:30
9. Matthew 23:25-26
10. Luke 11:39-41
11. Mark 4:28
12. Luke 10:5-6
13. Luke 14:28
14. Luke 14:31

9. THE HOLY SPIRIT

If any man thirst, let him come unto me and drink. He that believes on me, as the scripture has said, out of his belly shall flow rivers of living water. (But this He spoke of the Spirit, which they that believe on him should receive: for the Holy Ghost was not yet given because that Jesus was not yet glorified.)[1] Yes, the Comforter, which is the Holy Ghost, who the Father will send in my name, will teach you all things, and bring all things that I have said to you, to your remembrance.[2]

Nevertheless, I tell you the truth, it is expedient for you that I go away: for if I don't go away, the Comforter will not come to you; but if I depart, I will send him to you. And when he comes, he will convict the world of sin, and of righteousness, and of judgement: Of sin, because they don't believe on me; Of righteousness, because I go to my Father, and you see me no more; Of judgement, because the prince of this world is judged.[3]

When the Spirit of Truth comes, he will guide you into all truth: for he will not speak of himself; but whatever he hears, that will he speak: and he will show you things to come. He will glorify me, by taking what is mine and revealing it to you.[4] And I will pray to the Father, and He will give you another Comforter, that He may abide with you forever; even the Spirit of Truth; whom the world cannot receive, because it can't see him, neither know him: but you know him; for he dwells with you, and will be in you.[5] Yes, you will receive power, after the Holy Ghost has come upon you: and you will be witnesses unto me both in Jerusalem, and in all Judea, and in Samaria, and to the uttermost part of the earth.[6]

Wherefore I say unto you, All manner of sin and blasphemy shall be forgiven unto men: but the blasphemy against the Holy Ghost shall not be forgiven unto men. And whoever speaks a word against the Son of man, it shall be forgiven him: but whoever speaks against the Holy Ghost, it shall not be forgiven him, neither in this world, neither in the world to come.[7]

If a son shall ask bread of any of you that is a father, will he give him a stone? or if he ask a fish, will he for a fish give him a serpent? Or if he shall ask an egg, will he offer him a scorpion? If you then, being evil, know how to give good gifts to your children: how much more shall your heavenly Father give the Holy Spirit to them that ask him?[8] Go therefore, and teach all nations, baptizing them in the name of the Father and of the Son, and of the Holy Ghost.[9]

References:
1. John 7:37-39
2. John 14:26
3. John 16:7-11
4. John 16:13-14
5. John 14:16-17
6. Acts 1:8
7. Matthew 12:31-32
8. Luke 11:11-13
9. Matthew 28:19

10. WARNINGS

Beware of the leaven of the Pharisees and of the Sadducees,[1] which is hypocrisy.[2] Beware of the scribes, which love to go in long clothing, and love greetings in the market places, and the important seats in the synagogues, and the uppermost rooms at feasts: Which devour widows' houses, and for a pretence make long prayers: these shall receive greater damnation.[3]

Take heed to what you hear: with what measure you give out, it will be measured to you: and to you that hear will more be given.[4] Therefore, take heed how you hear: for whoever has, to him shall be given; and whoever has not, from him shall be taken even that which he seems to have.[5]

The light of the body is the eye: therefore when your eye is pure, your whole body is full of light; but when your eye is evil, your body is full of darkness. Take heed, therefore that the light which is in you, is not darkness.[6] And beware of covetousness: for a man's life does not consist in the abundance of things which he possesses.[7] Take heed, lest at any time your hearts be weighted down with carousing, drunkenness, and cares of this life, so that day come upon you unaware. For as a snare shall it come on all them that dwell on the face of the whole earth.[8] Remember, God knows your hearts: for that which is highly esteemed among man is an abomination in the sight of God.[9]

And know this, that if the goodman of the house had known what hour the thief would come, he would have watched, and not have allowed his house to be broken through. Therefore you be ready also: for the Son of man comes at an hour when you think not. Who then is that faithful and wise steward, whom his lord shall make ruler over his household, to give them their portion of meat in due season? Blessed is that servant, whom his lord when he comes shall find so doing. Of a truth I say unto you, that he will make him ruler over all that he has. But and if that servant say in his heart, My lord delays his coming; and shall begin to beat the menservants and maidens, and to eat and drink, and to be drunken; The lord of that servant will come in a day when he is not looking for him, and at an hour when he is not aware, and will cut him in pieces, and will appoint him his portion with the unbelievers. And that servant, which knew his lord's will, and prepared not himself, neither did according to his will, shall be beaten with many stripes. But he that knew not, and did commit things worthy of stripes, shall be beaten with few stripes. For unto whomever much is given, of him shall be much required: and to whom men have committed much, of him they will ask the more.[10]

Beware of false prophets, which come to you in sheep's clothing, but inwardly they are ravening wolves. You will know them by their fruits. Do men gather grapes of thorns, or figs of thistles? Even so every good tree brings forth good fruit; but a corrupt tree brings forth evil fruit. a good tree cannot bring forth evil fruit, neither can a corrupt tree bring forth good fruit. Every tree that brings not forth good fruit is cut down, and cast into the fire. Wherefore by their fruits you will know them. Be not deceived: for many will come in my name, saying, I am Christ; and the time draws near: Therefore don't follow after them.[12]

Take heed that you don't do your good deeds before men, to be seen of them: otherwise you will have no reward from your Father which is in heaven. Therefore, when you do your good deeds, do not sound a trumpet in front of you, like the hypocrites do in the synagogues and in the streets, that they may have the praise of men. Truly, I tell you, they have their reward.[13] And whoever exalts himself will be humbled; and he that humbles himself will be exalted.[14]

Do not despise one of these little ones; for I tell you, that in heaven their angels do always behold the face of my Father which is in heaven.[15] Have you ever read in the scriptures, The stone which the builders rejected, the same has become the head of the corner: this is the Lord's doing, and it is marvelous in our eyes? And whoever will fall on this stone will be broken: but on whoever it falls, it will grind him to powder.[16] Whoever therefore will be ashamed of me and of my words in this adulterous and sinful generation; of him also shall the Son of man be ashamed; when he comes in the glory of his Father with the holy angels.[17]

Sin no more, lest a worse thing come upon you[18] and remember, all who are in the graves will hear His voice, and come forth; they that have done good, unto the resurrection of life; and they that have done evil, unto the resurrection of damnation.[19] I am from above and if you do not believe that I am He, you will die in your sins.[20] And every idle word that men shall speak, they will give account of in the day of judgement. For by your words you will be justified, and by your words you will be condemned.[21]

References:
1. Matthew 16:6
2. Luke 12:1
3. Mark 12:38-40
4. Mark 4:24
5. Luke 8:18
6. Luke 11:34-35
7. Luke 12:15
8. Luke 21:34-35
9. Luke 16:15
10. Luke 12:39-48
11. Matthew 7:15-20
12. Luke 21:8
13. Matthew 6:1-2
14. Matthew 23:12
15. Matthew 18:10
16. Matthew 21:42 & 44
17. Mark 8:38
18. John 5:14
19. John 5:28-29
20. John 8:23-24
21. Matthew 12:36-37

11. REWARDS AND PROMISES

When you do good deeds, don't let your left hand know what your right hand is doing, so your good deeds may be in secret: and your Father which sees in secret, will himself reward you openly.[1] And when you pray, go in your closet, and when you shut the door, pray to your Father in secret, and your Father who sees in secret, will reward you openly.[2] But when you fast, anoint your head, and wash your face, so it won't look like you are fasting to other people, only to your Father, which sees in secret, and He will reward you openly.[3]

He that receives a prophet in the name of a prophet will receive a prophets reward; and he that receives a righteous man in the name of a righteous man will receive a righteous mans reward. And whoever gives a cold drink of water to one of these little ones only in the name of a disciple, truly I tell you, he will in no way, lose his reward.[4]

Blessed and happy are you, when men hate you, and separate you from their company,[5] speaking all manner of evil against you falsely, for my sake.[6] Rejoice in that day, and leap for joy: for behold, your reward is great in heaven, for so they persecuted the prophets which were before you.[8] But love your enemies, and do good, and lend, hoping for nothing again; and your reward will be great, and you will be the children of the Highest: for he is kind to the unthankful and to the evil.[9]

Come unto me, all of you who labor and are burdened, and I will give you rest. Take my yoke upon you, and learn of me; for I am meek and lowly in heart: and you will find rest for your souls. For my yoke is easy and my burden light.[10] And whoever drinks of the water that I give, will never thirst; but the water I give will be in you a well of water springing up into everlasting life.[11] I am the living bread which came down from heaven: if any man eat of this bread, he will live for ever.[12]

I will give you the keys of the kingdom of heaven; and whatever you bind on earth, will be bound in heaven; and whatever you loose on earth, will be loosed in heaven.[13] Behold, I give you power to tread on serpents and scorpions, and over all the power of the enemy: and nothing will by any means hurt you.[14] And I will give you words and wisdom, which all your adversaries will not be able to gainsay nor resist.[15]

For the Son of man shall come in the glory of his Father with his angels; and then he shall reward every man according to his works.[16] Then shall the King say unto them on his right hand, Come, you blessed of my Father, inherit the kingdom prepared for you from the foundation of the world: For I was hungry, and you gave me meat: I was thirsty, and you gave me drink: I was a stranger, and you took me in: Naked, and you clothed me: I was sick, and you visited me: I was in prison, and you came to me. Then shall the righteous answer him, saying, Lord, when did we see you hungry, and feed you? or thirsty, and gave you drink?

When did we see you as a stranger, and take you in? or naked, and clothed you? Or when did we see you sick, or in prison, and come to you? And the King shall answer and say unto them, Truly I say unto you, Inasmuch as you have done it unto one of the least of these my brothers, you have done it to me.[17] And whoever gives you a cup of water to drink in my name, because you belong to Christ, truly I tell you, he will not lose his reward.[18]

Truly I tell you, There is no man that has left house, or brothers, or sisters, or father, or mother, or wife, or children, or lands, for my sake, and the gospel's, but he shall receive a hundredfold now in this time, houses, and brothers, and sisters, and mothers, and children, and lands, with persecutions; and in the world to come eternal life.[19] In my Father's house are many mansions: if it were not so, I would have told you. I go to prepare a place for you. And if I go and prepare a place for you, I will come again, and receive you unto myself; that where I am, there ye may be also.[20]

I will pray to the Father, and he will give you another Comforter, that he may live with you forever.[21] Yes, Peace I leave with you, my peace I give to you; not as the world gives do I give to you. Let not your heart be troubled, neither let it be afraid.[22] And all things, whatever you ask in prayer, believing, you will receive.[23] Before now, you asked for nothing in my name: ask and you will receive, that your joy may be full.[24]

And remember, when you make a feast, call the poor, the maimed, the lame and the blind: And you will be blessed; for they cannot repay you: and you will be repaid at the resurrection of the just.[25]

He that has an ear, let him hear what the Spirit says to the churches; To him that overcomes will I give to eat of the tree of life,[26] and of the hidden manna, and will give him a white stone, and in the stone, a new name written, which no man knows but he that receives it.[27] He will not be hurt of the second death,[28] nor will I blot his name out of the book of life, but I will confess his name before my Father, and before his angels, and he will be clothed in white garments.[29] Him will I make a pillar in the temple of my God, and he will go no more out: and I will write upon him the name of my God, and the name of the city of my God, which is new Jerusalem.[30] He that overcomes and keeps my works to the end, will I give power over the nations[31] and I will give him the morning star.[32] To him that overcomes will I grant to sit with me in my throne.[33] And behold I come quickly; and my reward is with me, to give every man according as his work shall be.[34]

References:
1. Matthew 6:3-4
2. Matthew 6:6
3. Matthew 6:17-18
4. Matthew 10:41-42
5. Luke 6:22
6. Matthew 5:11
7. Luke 6:23
8. Matthew 5:12
9. Luke 6:35
10. Matthew 11:28-30
11. John 4:14
12. John 6:51
13. Matthew 16:19
14. Luke 10:19
15. Luke 21:15
16. Matthew 16:27
17. Matthew 25:34-40
18. Mark 9:41
19. Mark 10:29-30
20. John 14:2-3

12. HIS COMMANDS AND INSTRUCTIONS

He that has my commandments, and keeps them, is he that loves me: and he that loves me will be loved by my Father, and I will love him and reveal myself to him.[1]

Let your light so shine before men, that they may see your good works, and glorify your Father which is in heaven.[2] You have heard it said by them of old, "Thou shalt not kill"; and whoever kills will be in danger of the judgement: But I tell you, That whoever is angry with his brother without cause is in danger of the judgement: whoever insults his brother will be in danger of the council, and whoever says "You Fool" will be in danger of hell fire.[3]

Therefore if you bring your gift to the alter, and there remember, that your brother has something against you; leave your gift before the alter, and go first be reconciled to your brother, and then come and offer your gift.[4]

Agree with your adversary quickly, before you get to court, lest at any time the adversary deliver you to the judge, and the judge orders you to prison, where you will remain until you have paid the very last penny.[5] If any man will sue you at the law, and take away your coat, let him have your cloak also.[6]

You have heard it said by them of old, "Thou shalt

39

not commit adultery": But I tell you, that whoever looks upon a woman to lust after her has already committed adultery with her in his heart. So if your right eye causes you to sin, gouge it out, and throw it away: For it is better for you to lose one of your body parts, than to have your whole body cast into hell.[7]

You have also heard it said, "Do not break your oaths, but perform them to the Lord". But I tell you, Swear not at all; neither by heaven; for it is God's throne: Nor by the earth; for it is his footstool: neither by Jerusalem; for it is the city of the great king. Neither swear by your head, because you cannot make one hair black or white. But let your communication be, yea, yea; nay, nay: for whatever is more than this comes from evil.[8]

You have heard it said, "An eye for an eye, and a tooth for a tooth": But I tell you not to resist evil: but whoever will hit you on the right cheek, turn to him the other also.[9] And whoever compels you to go a mile, go two miles with him. Give to him that asks you, and don't turn your back on him that would borrow.[10]

You have heard it said, Love your neighbor and hate your enemy. But I tell you, Love your enemies, bless them that curse you, do good to them that hate you, and pray for them which despitefully use you, and persecute you.[11] Be perfect therefore even as your Father which is in heaven is perfect.[12]

Judge not, and you will not be judged: condemn not, and you will not be condemned: Forgive and you will be forgiven: Give and it will be given to you; good measure, pressed down, shaken together and running over will men give into your bosom. For with the same measure that you measure out, it will be measured to you again.[13] And why look at the speck in your brother's eye, but ignore the log in your own eye. How can you say, Let me remove the speck from your eye, when there is a log in your own eye. You hypocrite, first remove the log from your eye, so you can see clearly, then remove the speck from your brother's eye.[14]

Be merciful as your Father also is merciful,[15] doing good, lending, hoping for nothing again; and your reward shall be great, and you will be the children of the Highest: for he is kind to the unthankful and to the evil.[16]

If any man will come after me, let him deny himself, and take up his cross daily, and follow me.[17] Yes if any man serve me, let him follow me, and where I am, there will my servant be: if any man serve me, him will my Father honor.[18] Whoever does not bear his cross, and come after me, forsaking all that he has, cannot be my disciple.[19] If any man comes to me, and hates not his father, and mother, and wife, and children, and brothers, and sisters, yes, and his own life also, cannot be my disciple.[20] There is no man that has left house, or brothers, or sisters, or father, or mother, or wife, or children, or lands, for my sake, and the gospels, but he will receive a hundredfold now in this time, houses, and brothers, and sisters, and mothers, and children, and lands, with persecutions; and in the world to come, eternal life.[21]

If your brother trespass against you, rebuke him; and if he repent, forgive him. And if he trespass against you seven times in a day, and seven times in a day, turns to you and repents; you should forgive him.[22] Moreover if your brother trespasses against you, go and tell him his fault between just you and him: if he listens to you, you have gained your brother. But if he will not listen to you, then take with you one or two more, that in the mouth of two or three witnesses every word may be established. And if he refuses to listen to them, tell it to the church, and let him be unto you as a heathen and a tax collector.[23]

Know this, that if the owner of the house had known when the thief would come, he would have watched and not allowed his house to be broken up. Therefore, you also, should be ready, for at a time that you think not, the Son of man will come.[24] Then shall the King say to them on his right hand, Come, you blessed of my Father, inherit the kingdom prepared for you from the foundation of the world. For I was hungry and you gave me meat, I was thirsty, and you gave me a drink, I was a stranger, and you took me in, naked, and you clothed me, I was sick and you visited me, I was in prison and you came to me.[25] Inasmuch as you have done it unto the least of these my brothers, you have done it unto me.[26]

Abide in me, and I in you. As the branch cannot bear fruit of itself, unless it abides in the vine, neither can you, unless you abide in me. I am the vine, you are the branches: He that abides in me, and I in him, brings forth much fruit: for without me you can do nothing.[27] If you abide in me, and my words abide in you, you shall ask what you will, and it will be done for you.[28]

This my commandment, that you love one another, as I have loved you.[29] By this will all men know that you are my disciples, if you have love one to another.[30] If you love me, keep my commandments.[31] If you continue in my word, then you are my disciples indeed; and you will know the truth, and the truth will make you free.[32]

When you are invited to a wedding, don't sit in a place of honor, lest a more honored guest is invited and the host asks you to give up your seat for him, and then you in shame take the lowest place. But when you are invited, sit in the lowest place, that when the host comes, he may invite you to sit in a place of honor, and be honored in the presence of all who sit at your table. For whoever exalts himself will be abased; and he that humbles himself will be exalted.[33] And when you make a feast, call the poor, the maimed, the lame and the blind, and you will be blessed; for they cannot repay you; and you will be repaid at the resurrection of the just.[34]

Do to others as you would have them do back to you.[35] And whoever will save his life shall lose it: and whoever will lose his life for my sake will find it.[36] So come unto me, all you that labor and are heavy burdened, and I will give you rest. Take my yoke upon you, and learn of me; for I am meek and lowly of heart, and you will find rest for your souls. For my yoke is easy and my burden is light.[37]

Watch, and pray always,[38] that you enter not into temptation[39] and that you may be counted worthy to escape all these things that will come to pass, and to stand before the Son of man.[38] Let not your heart be troubled,[40] neither let it be afraid:[41] you believe in God, believe also in me.[40]

Don't be called Rabbi for one is your Master, even Christ; and you are all brothers. And call no man on earth your father: for one is your Father, which is in heaven. Neither be called masters, for one is your Master, even Christ. The greatest among you shall be called a servant.[42] Have salt in yourselves, and have peace with one another.[43]

When you have done all those things which are commanded of you, say, "We are unworthy servants, we have only done our duty."[44] If you do whatever I command you, you are my friends.[45] Go therefore, and teach all nations, to obey all things that I have commanded you; and, lo, I am with you always, even unto the end of the world. Amen.[46]

References:
1. John 14:21
2. Matthew 5:16
3. Matthew 5:21-22
4. Matthew 5:23-24
5. Matthew 5:25-26
6. Matthew 5:40
7. Matthew 5:27-29
8. Matthew 5:33-37
9. Matthew 5:38-39
10. Matthew 5:41-42
11. Matthew 5:43-44
12. Matthew 5:48
13. Luke 6:37-38
14. Matthew 7:3-5
15. Luke 6:36
16. Luke 6:35
17. Luke 9:23
18. John 12:26
19. Luke 14:27 & 33
20. Luke 14:26
21. Mark 10:29-30
22. Luke 17:3-4
23. Matthew 18:15-17
24. Matthew 24:43-44
25. Matthew 25:34-36
26. Matthew 25:40
27. John 15:4-5
28. John 15:7

29. John 15:12
30. John 13:35
31. John 14:15
32. John 8:31-32
33. Luke 14:8-11
34. Luke 14:13-14
35. Luke 6:31
36. Matthew 16:25
37. Matthew 11:28-30
38. Luke 21:36
39. Luke 22:40
40. John 14:1
41. John 14:27
42. Matthew 23:8-11
43. Mark 9:50
44. Luke 17:10
45. John 15:14
46. Matthew 28:19-20

13. MONEY AND MATERIALISM

Lay not up for yourselves treasures on earth, where moth and rust corrupt, and where thieves break through and steal. But lay up for yourselves treasures in heaven, where neither moth nor rust corrupts, and where thieves do not break through and steal: For where your treasure is, there will your heart be also.[1] Take heed, and beware of covetousness, for a man's life consists not in the abundance of the things which he possesses.[2]

The ground of a certain rich man brought forth plentifully, and he thought within himself, "What shall I do, because I have no room where to store my fruits?" And he said, This is what I will do; I will pull down my barns, and build greater; and there store all my fruits and goods. And I will say to my soul, Soul, you have many goods laid up for many years; take your ease, eat, drink, and be merry." But God said to him, You fool, this night your soul is required of you: then whose shall these things be, which you possess? So is he that lays up treasure for himself, and is not rich toward God.[3]

Therefore, I tell you, Take no thought for your life, what you shall eat,[4] drink or wear.[5] The life is more than meat, and the body is more than clothing. Consider the ravens; for they neither sow nor reap; and have neither storehouse nor barn; and God feeds them: how much more are you better than the fowls? And which of you with taking thought can add to his stature one cubit? If you are not able to do that thing which is least, why take thought for the rest? Consider the lilies, how they grow; they toil not, neither spin; and yet I tell you, that Solomon in all his glory was not dressed like one of these. If God so clothes the grass, which is today in the field, and tomorrow cast into the oven; how much more will he clothe you, O ye of little faith?[6]

Seek not what you will eat or drink, neither be of a doubtful mind. For all these things do the nations of the world seek after: and your Father knows that you have need of these things.[7] But seek first the kingdom of God and his righteousness; and all these things will be added to you. Take therefore no thought for tomorrow: for tomorrow shall take thought for the things of itself. Sufficient unto the day is the evil thereof.[8]

Use riches to gain friends that, when you run out, they may receive you into everlasting dwellings. He that is faithful in that which is least is faithful also in much: and he that is unjust in the least is also unjust in much. If therefore, you have not been faithful in the unrighteous riches, who will commit to your trust the true riches? And if you have not been faithful in that which is another man's who will give you that which is your own? No servant can serve two masters: for either he will hate the one, and love the other; or else he will be devoted to the one, and despise the other. You cannot serve God and mammon.[9] For where your treasure is, there will your heart be also.[10]

Labor not for the meat which perishes, but for that

meat which endures unto life everlasting, which the Son of man will give to you: for him has God the Father sealed.[11] But give, and it shall be given to you; good measure, pressed down, shaken together and running over, will men give into your bosom. For with the same measure that you give out, it shall be measured back to you again.[12] And unto you that hear shall more be given. For he that has, to him shall be given: and he that has not, from him shall be taken even that which he has.[13]

The deceitfulness of riches,[14] and the pleasures of this life,[15] entering in, choke the word and you become unfruitful,[14] bringing no fruit to perfection.[15] Children, how hard it is for them that trust in riches to enter into the kingdom of God![16] If you want to be perfect, go and sell what you have, and give to the poor, and you will have treasure in heaven: and come and follow me.[17] But no man has left house, or brothers, or sisters, or father, or mother, or wife, or children, or lands, for my sake, and the gospel's, but he shall receive a hundredfold now in this time, houses, and brothers, and sisters, and mothers, and children, and lands, with persecutions; and in the world to come, eternal life. But many that are first will be last; and the last first.[18]

Woe unto you, Scribes and Pharisees, hypocrites! For you pay tithe of mint[19] and all manner of herbs,[20] and have omitted the weightier matters of the law, judgement, mercy, faith[19] and the love of God: these you ought to have done, as well as the other.[20]

References:

1. *Matthew 6:19-21*
2. *Luke 12:15*
3. *Luke 12:16-21*
4. *Matthew 6:25*
5. *Matthew 6:31*
6. *Luke 12:22-28*
7. *Luke 12:29-30*
8. *Matthew 6:33-34*
9. *Luke 16:9-13*
10. *Luke 12:34*
11. *John 6:27*
12. *Luke 6:38*
13. *Mark 4:24-25*
14. *Mark 4:19*
15. *Luke 8:14*
16. *Mark 10:24*
17. *Matthew 19:21*
18. *Mark 10:29-31*
19. *Matthew 23:23*
20. *Luke 11:42*

14. MARRIAGE AND DIVORCE

And the Pharisees came to Jesus, to test him, and asked him, "Is it lawful to divorce one's wife for any cause?" And Jesus answered them, What did Moses command you? And they said, Moses permitted them to write a bill of divorce and put her away.[1]

Jesus answered, For the hardness of your heart he wrote you this precept,[2] but have you not read, that he which made them at the beginning[3] of the creation[4] made them male and female,[3] And said, For this cause shall a man leave father and mother and cleave to his wife: and they two shall be one flesh.[5]

Therefore, they are no more two, but one flesh. What God therefore has joined together, let not man put asunder.[6] Moses, because of the hardness of your hearts allowed you to divorce your wives: but from the beginning it was not so. And I tell you, Whoever divorces his wife except it be for fornication, and shall marry another, commits adultery: and whoever marries her which is divorced, commits adultery.[7] And if a woman divorces her husband, and be married to another, she commits adultery.[8]

The children of this world marry, and are given in marriage: But they which shall be counted worthy to obtain that world, and the resurrection from the dead, neither marry, nor are given in marriage.[9]

References:
1. Mark 10:2-4
2. Mark 10:5
3. Matthew 19:4
4. Mark 10:6
5. Matthew 19:5
6. Matthew 19:6
7. Matthew 19:8-9
8. Mark 10:12
9. Luke 20:34-35

15. THE HEART OF MAN

A good man out of the good treasure of his heart brings forth that which is good; and an evil man out of the evil treasure of his heart brings forth that which is evil: for of the abundance of the heart, the mouth speaks.[1]

There is nothing from without, that entering into a man, can defile him: but the things which come out of him, those are what defile a man.[2] This is because, things from without, do not enter his heart, but into the belly, and then out again.[3]

What comes out of the man, makes him unclean, for from within, out of the heart of man, proceed evil thoughts, adulteries, fornications, murders, thefts, covetousness, wickedness, deceit,[4] false witness,[5] lasciviousness, an evil eye, blasphemy, pride and foolishness: All these evil things come from within, and defile the man.[4]

You should love the lord your God with all your heart, and with all your soul, and all your mind, and with all your strength. Yes to love him with all the heart, and with all the understanding, and with all the soul, and with all the strength, and to love his neighbor as himself, is more than all whole burnt offerings and sacrifice.[6]

Blessed are the pure in heart: for they shall see God.[7] And God knows your hearts, for that which is highly esteemed among men is an abomination in the sight of God.[8] So don't fear them which kill the body but are not able to kill the soul: but rather fear him who is able to destroy both soul and body in hell.[9] So take heed, lest at any time your hearts be weighed down with squanderous living and drunkenness, and the cares of this life, and so the day come upon you unawares.[10]

A good tree does not bring forth corrupt fruit; neither does a corrupt tree bring forth good fruit. For every tree is known by his own fruit. For of thorns men do not gather figs, nor of a bramble bush do they gather grapes.[11]

Remember, where your treasure is, there will your heart be also.[12]

References:
1. Luke 6:45
2. Mark 7:15
3. Mark 7:19
4. Mark 7:20-23
5. Matthew 15:19
6. Mark 12:30 & 33
7. Matthew 5:8
8. Luke 16:15
9. Matthew 10:28
10. Luke 21:34
11. Luke 6:43-44
12. Luke 12:34

16. YOUR WORDS

Every word that men shall speak, they will give account of in the day of judgement. For by your words you are justified and by your words you will be condemned.[1] Therefore whatever you have spoken in darkness shall be heard in the light; and that which you have whispered in the closets shall be proclaimed upon the housetops. For there is nothing covered, that shall not be revealed; neither hid, that shall not be known.[2]

And whoever speaks a word against the Son of man, it will be forgiven him: but whoever speaks against the Holy Ghost, it will not be forgiven him, neither in this world, nor in the world to come.[3]

It is not that which goes into the mouth that defiles a man, but that which comes out of the mouth, this defiles a man.[4] Whatever enters in at the mouth goes into your belly, then out of your body.[5] But those things which proceed out of the mouth come forth from the heart; and they defile the man. For out of the heart proceed evil thoughts, murders, adulteries, fornications, thefts, false witness, blasphemies[6] covetousness, wickedness, deceit, lasciviousness, an evil eye, pride and foolishness. All these things come from within, and defile the man.[7]

A good man out of the good treasure of his heart brings forth that which is good; and an evil man out of the evil treasure of his heart brings forth that which is evil: for of the abundance of the heart his mouth speaks.[8] No man which does a miracle in my name, can soon after speak evil of me.[9] And he that speaks of himself seeks his own glory.[10] But whoever shall insult his brother will be in danger of the council and whoever shall say "you fool" shall be in danger of hell fire.[11]

Truly I tell you, that whoever shall say to this mountain, Be removed and cast into the sea; and shall not doubt in his heart, but shall believe that those things which he says will come to pass; he shall have whatever he says.[12]

References:
1. *Matthew 12:36-37*
2. *Luke 12:2-3*
3. *Matthew 12:32*
4. *Matthew 15:11*
5. *Matthew 15:17*
6. *Matthew 15:18-19*
7. *Mark 7:22-23*
8. *Luke 6:45*
9. *Mark 9:39*
10. *John 7:18*
11. *Matthew 5:22*
12. *Mark 11:23*

17. CONCERNING GOD'S WILL

My food and nourishment is to do the will of him that sent me, and to finish his work.[1] I can of my own self do nothing: as I hear, I judge: and my judgement is just; because I seek not my will, but the will of the Father which sent me.[2]

For I came down from heaven, not to do my will, but the will of him that sent me. And this is the Father's will which sent me, that all of which he has given me, I should lose nothing, but raise it up again at the last day. And that every one which sees the Son, and believes on him, may have everlasting life: and I will raise him up at the last day.[3] It is not the will of your Father which is in heaven, that one of these little ones should perish.[4]

Not every one that says to me, Lord, Lord, will enter the kingdom of heaven; but he that does the will of my Father which is in heaven.[5] For whoever shall do the will of my Father which is in heaven, the same is my brother, sister and mother.[6] Yes, my mother and brothers are these which hear the word of God, and do it.[7]

He that enters in by the door is the shepherd of the sheep, and the sheep hear his voice: and he calls his sheep by name, and leads them out. He goes before them, and the sheep follow him: for they know his voice. And a stranger they will not follow, but will flee from him: for they don't know the voice of strangers.[8]

Howbeit when he, the Spirit of truth, is come, he will guide you into all truth: for he will not speak of himself; but whatever he hears, that shall he speak: and he will show you things to come. He will glorify me, for he will take what is mine and reveal it to you.[9]

A Parable

The servant which knew his lord's will, and prepared not himself, neither did according to his will, shall be beaten with many stripes. But he that didn't know, and did commit things worthy of stripes, will be beaten with few stripes. For unto whoever much is given, of him shall much be required: and to whom men have committed much, of him they will ask the more.[10]

References:
1. John 4:34
2. John 5:30
3. John 6:38-40
4. Matthew 18:14
5. Matthew 7:21
6. Matthew 12:50
7. Luke 8:21
8. John 10:2-5
9. John 16:13-14
10. Luke 12:47-48

18. FORGIVENESS AND RECONCILIATION

When you stand praying, forgive, if you have ought against any: that your Father which is in heaven may forgive you your trespasses. But if you do not forgive, neither will your Father which is in heaven forgive your trespasses.[1] If you bring your gift to the alter, and there remember that your brother has ought against you, leave your gift before the alter, and go first be reconciled to your brother, and then come and offer your gift.[2]

Judge not, and you shall not be judged, condemn not, and you shall not be condemned: forgive, and you shall be forgiven.[3] If your brother trespass against you seven times in a day, and seven times in a day turn again to you, saying, "I repent"; you should forgive him.[4] Peter asked, how often he should forgive his brother-until seven times? Then Jesus answered, I tell you, not until seven times, but until seventy times seven.[5]

Therefore is the kingdom of heaven like unto a certain king, which would take account of his servants. And when he began to assess, one was brought to him, which owed ten thousand talents. But when he could not pay, the king commanded him to be sold, and his wife, and children, and all that he had, and payment to be made. The servant fell down, worshipping him, saying, Lord, have patience with me, and I will repay all. Then the lord of that servant was moved with compassion, and loosed him, and forgave him the debt.[6]

But the same servant went out and found one of his fellowservants, which owed him one hundred pence: and he laid his hands on him, and took him by the throat, saying, Pay me what you owe. And his fellowservant fell down at his feet, and besought him, saying, Have patience with me, and I will repay all. But he would not listen to him, and went and cast him into prison, till he should pay the debt.[7]

So when his fellowservants saw what was done, they were very sorry, and came and told the king all that was done. Then the king, after he called him, said to him, "You wicked servant, I forgave you all that debt, because you pleaded with me. Shouldn't you also have had compassion on your fellowservant, even as I had pity on you? And the king was very angry, and delivered him to the tormentors, till he should pay all that was due him. So likewise will my heavenly Father do also to you, if you from your hearts don't forgive every brother that trespasses against you.[8]

References:
1. Mark 11:25-26   2. Matthew 5:23-24
3. Luke 6:37   4. Luke 17:4
5. Matthew 18:21-22   6. Matthew 18:23-27
7. Matthew 18:28-30   8. Matthew 18:31-35

19. CHILDREN

Except you be converted, and become as little children, you will not enter into the kingdom of heaven. Whoever therefore shall humble himself like this little child, the same is the greatest in the kingdom of heaven.[1]

Whoever receives a child like this in my name, receives me: and whoever receives me, is really receiving him that sent me. And whoever causes one of these little ones who believe in me to sin, it would be better for him that a millstone were hanged about his neck, and he were cast into the sea[2] and drown in the depths of it.[3]

Woe to the world for the temptations that lead people to sin. Such things must come, but woe to the man by whom they come![4] Take heed that you don't despise one of these little ones; for I tell you, That in heaven, their angels do always behold the face of my Father which is in heaven.[5] It is not the will of your Father which is in heaven, that one of these little ones should perish.[6]

When young children were brought to Jesus, that he might put his hands on them and pray, the disciples rebuked those that brought them.[7] When Jesus saw it, he was very displeased, and said to them, Allow the little children to come to me, and forbid them not: for of such is the kingdom of God. Truly I tell you, whoever will not receive the kingdom of God as a little child, will not enter in.

And Jesus took them in his arms, put his hands upon them, and blessed them.[8]

He that is least among you all, the same shall be great.[9]

References:
1. Matthew 18:3-4
2. Mark 9:37 & 42
3. Matthew 18:6
4. Matthew 18:7
5. Matthew 18:10
6. Matthew 18:14
7. Matthew 19:13
8. Mark 10:14-16
9. Luke 9:48

20. SEVEN PARADOXICAL TRUTHS

I. Whoever loves his life[1] and tries to save[2] or find it, will lose it.[3]

II. Whoever hates his life in this world,[1] losing it for my sake and the gospels,[4] will save,[5] find,[3] preserve[2] and keep it unto life eternal.[1]

III. Whoever will be chief among you, let him be your servant,[6] yes the chiefest will be the servant of all.[7]

IV. He that is greatest among you, let him be as the younger,[8] your minister[9] and servant,[10] for he that is least among you all, the same will be great.[11]

V. Many that are first shall be last; and the last first.[12] If any man desires to be first, he must be last of all, and servant of all.[13]

VI. Whoever exalts himself will be humbled; and whoever humbles himself will be exalted.[14]

VII. It is more blessed to give than to receive.[15]

References:

1. *John 12:25*
2. *Luke 17:33*
3. *Matthew 10:39*
4. *Mark 8:35*
5. *Luke 9:24*
6. *Matthew 20:27*
7. *Mark 10:44*
8. *Luke 22:26*
9. *Matthew 20:26*
10. *Matthew 23:11*
11. *Luke 9:48*
12. *Mark 10:31*
13. *Mark 9:35*
14. *Matthew 23:12*
15. *Acts 11:35*

21. HYPOCRISY, PHARISEES AND THE LAW

Think not that I have come to destroy the law, or the prophets: I am not come to destroy, but to fulfill. For truly I tell you, Till heaven and earth pass away, one jot or one tittle will in no way pass from the law, till all be fulfilled. Whoever breaks one of the least of these commandments, and teaches men so, shall be called the least in the kingdom of heaven; but whoever will do and teach them shall be called great in the kingdom of heaven.[1]

And one came to Jesus saying, Good Master, what good thing shall I do, that I may have eternal life? If you will enter into life, keep the commandments. Which? Jesus said, Thou shall do no murder, Thou shall not commit adultery, Thou shall not steal, Thou shall not bear false witness, Honor your father and mother: and Thou shall love your neighbor as yourself. The young man said, All these things have I kept from my youth up, what lack I yet? Jesus said, If you will be perfect, go and sell what you have, and give to the poor, and you will have treasure in heaven: and come and follow me.[2]

When one of the scribes heard them reasoning together he asked Jesus, "Which is the most important commandment of all"? And Jesus answered him, The first of all the commandments is, Hear, O Israel; The Lord our God is one Lord. And you should love the Lord your God with all your heart, and with all your soul, and with all your mind, and with all your strength: this is the first and most important commandment. And the second is similar, namely this, you should love your neighbor as yourself. There is no other commandment greater than these.[3] On these two commandments hang all the law and the prophets.[4]

The scribes and Pharisees said to Jesus, "Why do your disciples transgress the tradition of the elders? for they don't wash their hands when they eat. But Jesus answered, Why do you transgress the commandment of God with your traditions?[5] You hypocrites,[6] you draw near to God with your mouth, and honor Him with your lips; but your heart is far from Him. In vain you worship God, teaching the rules of men.[7]

The Pharisees asked Jesus, "Why do they do things on the sabbath day which are not lawful?" Jesus answered, Have you never read what David did, when he had need, and was hungry, he and they that were with him? How he went into the house of God and did eat the shewbread, which is not lawful to eat unless you were a priest, and gave some to those that were with him? The sabbath was made for man, man wasn't made for the sabbath. Therefore the Son of man is Lord also of the sabbath.[8]

It came to pass on another sabbath, there was a man in the synagogue with a withered hand. And Jesus said, Is it lawful on the sabbath days to do good, or to do evil? to save life or destroy it? Then after looking upon them, he said to the man; Stretch forth your hand. When he did, it was restored whole as the other. But the scribes and Pharisees were filled with anger.[9]

On another occasion, Jesus healed a bent over woman on the sabbath. And the ruler of the synagogue answered with indignation, because Jesus healed on the sabbath and said to the people: There are six days in which men ought to work: come and be healed on those days, but not on the sabbath. But Jesus answered, You hypocrite, does not each one of you on the sabbath loose his ox or his ass from the stall, and lead him away to watering? And ought not this woman, being a daughter of Abraham, whom Satan has bound these eighteen years, be loosed from this bond on the sabbath day? And when Jesus said this, all his adversaries were ashamed and the people rejoiced for all the glorious things done by him.[10]

Hypocrites love to pray standing where they can be seen by others. When they fast, they disfigure their faces, so others will know they are fasting. Truly, I tell you, they have their reward.[11] The pharisees give you heavy burdens and lay them on your shoulders but won't lift a finger to do them themselves. Any works that they do, are done to be noticed by others and they love the prominent seats at feasts or in the synagogues and to be greeted in the market and called, Rabbi, Rabbi.[12]

Woe unto you scribes and Pharisees, hypocrites, for you travel over land and sea to make a convert, then turn him into twice the child of hell you are.

You are fools, blind guides and hypocrites, for you tithe of even the smallest thing, but neglect the weightier matters of the law, judgement, mercy and faith. You should have done both. You strain at a gnat, and swallow a camel.[13]

The outside of your cup is clean, but within, you are full of extortion, excess[14] and ravening wickedness.[15] Clean the inside first, that your outside may be clean also[14] and give alms of such things as you have and all things will be clean to you.[16] Woe unto you, scribes and Pharisees, hypocrites! for you are like whitewashed tombs, which appear beautiful outwardly, but are full of dead mans bones, and all uncleanness within. Outwardly you appear righteous to men, but within you are full of hypocrisy and iniquity.[14] You serpents, you generation of vipers, how can you escape the damnation of hell? Behold, I send you prophets, wise men, and scribes: some of them you will kill and crucify, and some you will whip in your synagogues, and persecute from city to city: That upon you, may come all the righteous blood shed upon the earth.[17]

Beware of the leaven of the Pharisees, which is hypocrisy.[18] They lay aside the commandment of God, and obey the traditions of men,[19] making the word of God of no effect.[29] Every plant which my heavenly Father has not planted, will be rooted up.[21]

Woe unto you scribes and Pharisees, for you shut the kingdom of heaven in the faces of men; neither do you go in yourselves, neither do you allow them to enter who are trying. You hypocrites!

You take the homes of widows, then for a pretence, make long prayers: therefore you will receive the greater damnation.[22]

Except your righteousness exceed the righteousness of the scribes and Pharisees, you will in no case enter into the kingdom of heaven.[23]

References:
1. Matthew 5:17-19
2. Matthew 19:16-21
3. Mark 12:28-31
4. Matthew 22:40
5. Matthew 15:2-3
6. Matthew 15:7
7. Matthew 15:8-9
8. Mark 2:24-28
9. Luke 6:6-11
10. Luke 13:11-17
11. Matthew 6:5 & 16
12. Matthew 23:4-7
13. Matthew 23:15-24
14. Matthew 23:25-28
15. Luke 11:39
16. Luke 11:41
17. Matthew 23:33-35
18. Luke 12:1
19. Mark 7:8
20. Mark 7:13
21. Matthew 15:13
22. Matthew 23:13-14
23. Matthew 5:20

22. WORRY AND FEAR

You will hear of wars and rumors of wars: see that you are not troubled: for all these things must come to pass, but the end is not yet.[1] And fear not them which kill the body, but are not able to kill the soul: but rather fear him which is able to destroy both soul and body in hell.[2]

Are not two sparrows sold for a farthing? and not one of them falls to the ground without your Father knowing it. But the very hairs of your head are all numbered. Fear not therefore, you are of more value than many sparrows.[3]

Let not your heart be troubled, neither allow it to be afraid:[4] you believe in God, believe also in me.[5] Peace I leave with you, my peace I give to you: but not as the world gives.[4] So be not afraid, only believe[6]; for it is your Fathers good pleasure to give you the kingdom.[7]

Now it came to pass, as they went, that Jesus entered in to a certain village: and a certain woman named Martha, received him into her house. And she had a sister called Mary, who sat at Jesus' feet, and heard his word. But Martha was very busy with much serving, and came to him, and said, "Lord, do you not care that my sister has left me to work by myself? Tell her to come and help me." And Jesus answered and said, Martha,

Martha, you are anxious and upset about many things: But one thing is needful; and Mary has chosen the better part, and it will not be taken away from her.[8]

Take heed, lest the cares and worries of this life,[9] enter in and choke the word, becoming unfruitful,[10] and that day come upon you unawares.[9]

References:
1. Matthew 24:6
2. Matthew 10:28
3. Matthew 10:29-31
4. John 14:27
5. John 14:1
6. Mark 5:36
7. Luke 12:32
8. Luke 10:38-42
9. Luke 21:34

23. FAITH

If you can believe, all things are possible to him that believes.[1] **And the apostles said to the Lord, "Increase our faith." And Jesus replied,** If you had faith as a grain of mustard seed, you could say to this sycamine tree, Be plucked up by the root, and be planted in the sea; and it would obey you.[2]

Have faith in God, for truly I tell you, that whoever will say unto this mountain, Be removed, and be cast into the sea; and will not doubt in his heart, but shall believe that those things which he says will come to pass; he will have whatever he says. Therefore I tell you, the things you desire when you pray, believe that you receive them, and you will have them.[3] Have faith, and doubt not;[4] and nothing will be impossible to you.[5] All things that you ask in prayer, believing, you will receive.[6]

If then God so clothes the grass, which is today in the field and tomorrow cast into the oven; how much more will he clothe you, O you of little faith?[7] Be not afraid, only believe.[8]

When met with faith, Jesus said:
1) As you have believed, so be it done unto you.[9]
2) According to your faith be it unto you.[10]
3) Great is your faith: be it unto you as you desire.[11]
4) Daughter, your faith has made you whole; go in peace and be whole of your plague.[12]
5) Your faith has saved you; go in peace.[13]

One Example of Faith in Action

And a certain woman, which had an issue of blood twelve years, And had suffered many things of many physicians, and had spent all that she had, and was not any better, but rather grew worse, When she had heard of Jesus, came in the crowd behind, and touched his garment. For she said, If I may touch but his clothes, I shall be whole. And straightway the fountain of her blood was dried up; and she felt in her body that she was healed of that plague. And Jesus, immediately knowing in himself that power had gone out of him, turned around in the crowd and said, Who touched my clothes? And his disciples said unto him, "You see the multitude crowding you, and you say, Who touched me?" And he looked around about to see her that had done this thing. But the woman fearing and trembling, knowing what was done in her, came and fell down before him, and told him all the truth. And he said unto her, Daughter, your faith has made you whole; go in peace, and be whole of your plague.[19]

He that believes and is baptized shall be saved[15] and never die.[16] And these signs will follow them that believe; In my name they will cast out devils; they will speak with new tongues; They will take up serpents; and if they drink any deadly thing, it will not hurt them; they will lay hands on the sick, and they will recover.[17] Truly, I tell you, He that believes on me, the works that I do shall he do also; and greater works than these shall he do; because I go unto my Father.

References:
1. Mark 9:23
2. Luke 17:5-6
3. Mark 11:22-24
4. Matthew 21:21
5. Matthew 17:20
6. Matthew 21:22
7. Luke 12:28
8. Mark 5:36
9. Matthew 8:13
10. Matthew 9:29
11. Matthew 15:28
12. Mark 5:34
13. Luke 7:50
14. Mark 5:25-34
15. Mark 16:16
16. John 11:26
17. Mark 16:17-18

24. SOUL WINNING

It is written, and thus it behoved Christ to suffer, and to rise from the dead the third day: And that repentance and remission of sins should be preached in his name among all nations beginning at Jerusalem.[1] And whoever therefore will confess me before men, him will I confess also before my Father which is in heaven.[2]

You are the salt of the earth[3] and salt is good:[4] but if the salt has lost his savour, how will it be salted? It is good for nothing,[3] not fit for the land, nor the dung hill;[5] only to be cast out and walked on by men.[3] Every one will be salted with fire, and every sacrifice will be salted with salt.[6] Have salt in yourselves, and have peace with one another.[4]

You are the light of the world. A city that is set on a hill cannot be hid.[7] Neither do men light a candle, and cover it with a vessel, or put it under the bed[8] or some secret place, neither under a bushel,[9] but set it on a candlestick, that they which enter in may see the light[8] as well as those who are in the house.[10] Let your light so shine before men, that they may see your good works, and glorify your Father which is in heaven.[11]

Say not, there are yet four months, and then comes the harvest. Behold I tell you, Lift up your eyes, and look on the fields; for they are white already to harvest.[12] The harvest truly is plenteous, but the laborers are few; Pray therefore, that the

Lord of the harvest, will send forth labourers into his harvest.[13]

And he that reaps receives wages, and gathers fruit unto life eternal: that both he that sows and he that reaps may rejoice together. And herein is that saying true, One sows, and another reaps. I sent you to reap where you bestowed no labor: other men labored, and you are entered into their labors.[14]

All power is given unto me in heaven and in earth. Go therefore,[15] into all the world, and preach the gospel to every creature,[16] teaching all nations to observe all things I commanded you.[15] And he that believes and is baptized will be saved; but he that doesn't believe will be damned.[17] Baptize them in the name of the Father, and of the Son, and of the Holy Ghost,[15] and these signs will follow them that believe; In my name they will cast out devils; they will speak with new tongues; They will take up serpents; and if they drink any deadly thing, it will not hurt them; they will lay hands on the sick, and they will recover.[18]

And, lo, I am with you always, even unto the end of the world. Amen[15]

References:

1. Luke 24:46-47
2. Matthew 10:32
3. Matthew 5:13
4. Mark 9:50
5. Luke 14:35
6. Mark 9:49
7. Matthew 5:14
8. Luke 8:16
9. Luke 11:33
10. Matthew 5:15
11. Matthew 5:16
12. John 4:35
13. Matthew 9:37-38
14. John 4:36-38
15. Matthew 28:18-20
16. Mark 16:15
17. Mark 16:16
18. Mark 16:17-18

25. EVENTS TO OCCUR BETWEEN 1ST AND 2ND COMING

And as he sat upon the mount of Olives, the disciples came to Jesus privately, saying, "When shall these things be? and what will be the sign of your coming, and of the end of the world,[1] and when all these things will be fulfilled?"[2] And some spoke of the temple, how it was decorated with beautiful stones and gifts. And Jesus said, As for these things which you see, the days will come, in which there will not be left one stone upon another, that will not be thrown down.[3]

And Jesus answered and said unto them, Take heed that no man deceive you. For many will come in my name, saying, I am Christ,[4] and the time is very near: do not follow them.[5] And you will hear of wars,[6] commotions,[7] and rumors of wars, see that you don't become troubled[6] or terrified: for these things must first come to pass;[7] but the end is not yet.[6]

For nation will rise against nation, kingdom against kingdom: and there will be famines, plagues,[8] troubles[9] and earthquakes in many places; and fearful sights and great signs will there be from heaven.[10] All these are the beginning of sorrows.[11]

But before all these, they will lay their hands on you and persecute you, delivering you up to the synagogues, and into prisons, being brought before kings and rulers for my name's sake[12] and a testimony against them. You will be delivered up to councils, and be beaten[13] and afflicted and they will kill you.[14]

But when they lead you and deliver you up, take no thought beforehand what you will speak, and don't premeditate: but speak that which is given to you in that hour: for it is not you that speaks, but the Holy Ghost.[15] Then many will fall away from the faith, betraying and hating one another.[16] Now the brother will betray the brother to death, and the father the son; and children will rise up against their parents, and cause them to be put to death. And you will be hated of all men.[17]

Many false prophets will arise, deceiving many, and because iniquity will abound, the love of many will grow cold. He that endures to the end will be saved.[18] This gospel of the kingdom[19] must be published among all nations,[20] and preached in all the world for a witness unto all nations; and then will the end come.[19]

When you see Jerusalem surrounded with armies, then know that the desolation is soon.[21] When you see the abomination of desolation, spoken of by the prophet Daniel, standing in the holy place,[22] where it ought not, (let him that reads understand,) then let them that be in Judaea flee to the mountains.[23] Let them that are in the city depart; and let those in the country not enter the city.[24] Let him which is on the housetop not come down to take anything out of his house: neither let him which is in the field return back to take his clothes.[25] For these are the days of vengeance, that all things which are written may be fulfilled.[26]

But woe unto them that are pregnant or nursing their child! Pray that your flight is not in winter, nor on the sabbath day.[27] For there will be great distress in the land, and wrath upon this people.[28] For then there will be great tribulation[29] and affliction, such as was not from the beginning of the creation which God created unto this time, neither will be.[30]

And they will fall by the edge of the sword, and shall be led away captive into all nations: and Jerusalem will be trodden down of the Gentiles, until the times of the Gentiles be fulfilled.[31] And except the Lord shorten those days, no flesh would survive: but for the elect's sake, whom he has chosen, those days will be shortened.[32]

Then if any man will say to you, "Christ is here" or "Christ is there"; don't believe it. For there will arise false Christs, and false prophets, and will show great signs and wonders; so much that if it were possible to deceive[33] and seduce[34] the very elect.[33] But take heed: behold, I have foretold you all things.[35] Therefore, if they say to you, "Behold, he is in the desert; don't go there: Behold, he is in the secret chambers;" don't believe it.[36]

As the lightning comes out of the east, and shines even to the west; so also shall the coming of the Son of man be.[37] But first he must suffer many things, and be rejected of this generation. And as it was in the days of Noah, so shall it be also in the days of the Son of man. They ate and drank and married wives, and they were given in marriage, until the day that Noah entered into the ark, and the flood came, and destroyed them all.[38]

Likewise also as it was in the days of Lot; they did eat and drink, they bought, they sold, the planted, they built; But the same day that Lot went out of Sodom, it rained fire and brimstone from heaven, and destroyed them all. Even thus will it be in the day when the Son of man is revealed. In that day, he which is on the housetop, and his stuff is in the house, let him not come down to take it away: and he that is in the field, let him likewise not return back. Remember Lot's wife. Whoever will seek to save his life, will lose it; and whoever will lose his life, shall preserve it.[39]

I tell you, in that night there will be two men in one bed; the one will be taken, and the other left. Two women will be grinding together; the one will be taken and the other left. Two men will be in the field; the one will be taken and the other left.[40] Watch therefore: for you don't know what hour your Lord will come.[41] Of that day and hour no man knows, no, not the angels of heaven, but my Father only.[42]

But know this, that if the owner of the house had known at what time the thief would come, he would have watched, and would not have allowed his house to be broken up. Therefore, you also be ready: for in such an hour as you think not, the Son of man comes.[43]

And they answered and said, "Where, Lord?" And Jesus replied, Wherever the body is, there will the eagles be gathered together.[44]

Immediately after the tribulation of those days[45] there will be signs in the sun, and in the moon, and in the stars,[46] for the sun will be darkened, and the moon will not give her light, and the stars will fall from heaven, and the powers of the heavens will be shaken.[45] Upon the earth, there will be distress of nations, with perplexity; the sea and the waves roaring; Men's hearts failing them for fear, and for looking after those things which are coming on the earth.[46]

And then will appear the sign of the Son of man in heaven: and then will all the tribes of the earth mourn, and they will see the Son of man coming in the clouds of heaven with power and great glory. And he will send his angels with a great sound of a trumpet, and they shall gather together his elect from the four winds,[47] from the uttermost part of the earth, to the uttermost part of heaven.[48] And when these things begin to come to pass, then look up, and lift up your heads; your redemption draws near.[49]

Now learn a parable of the fig tree,[50] and all the trees;[51] When his branch is yet tender, and puts forth leaves, you know that summer is near.[50] So likewise, when you see these things come to pass, you know the kingdom of God is at hand,[52] even at the doors.[53] Truly I tell you, that this generation will not pass away, till all these things be fulfilled: Heaven and earth will pass away, but my words will not pass away.[54]

When the Son of man comes in all his glory, and all the holy angels with him, then will he sit upon the throne of his glory: And all nations will be gathered before him: and he will separate them from one another, as a shepherd divides his sheep from the goats: And he will set the sheep on his right hand, but the goats on the left. Then will the King say to them on his right hand, Come, you blessed of my Father, inherit the kingdom prepared for you from the foundation of the world.[55]

For I was hungry, and you gave me food: I was thirsty, and you gave me drink: I was a stranger, and you took me in: Naked, and you clothed me, I was sick and you visited me, I was in prison, and you came to me. Then shall the righteous answer him, saying, Lord, when did we see you hungry and feed you, or thirsty and give you drink? When did we see you as a stranger and take you in, or naked and clothe you? Or when did we see you sick, or in prison and come to you?[56]

And the King will answer and say to them, Truly I tell you, Inasmuch as you have done it to one of the least of these my brothers, you have done it unto me.[57]

Then shall he also say to them on the left hand, Depart from me, you cursed, into everlasting fire, prepared for the devil and his angels: For I was hungry and you didn't feed me, I was thirsty and you gave me no drink: I was a stranger, and you didn't take me in, naked and you didn't clothe me, sick and in prison, and you didn't visit me.[58]

Then shall they also answer him saying, Lord when did we see you hungry or thirsty, or a stranger, or naked, or sick, or in prison, and did not minister to you? Then shall he answer them, saying, Truly I tell you, Inasmuch as you did it not to one of the least of these, you did it not unto me.

And these will go away into everlasting punishment: but the righteous into life eternal.[59]

References:
1. Matthew 24:3
2. Mark 13:4
3. Luke 21:5-6
4. Matthew 25:4-5
5. Luke 21:8
6. Matthew 24:6
7. Luke 21:9
8. Matthew 24:7
9. Mark 13:8
10. Luke 21:11
11. Matthew 24:8
12. Luke 21:12
13. Mark 13:9
14. Matthew 24:9
15. Mark 13:11
16. Matthew 24:10
17. Mark 13:12-13
18. Matthew 24:11-13
19. Matthew 24:14
20. Mark 13:10
21. Luke 21:20
22. Matthew 24:15
23. Mark 13:14
24. Luke 21:21
25. Matthew 24:17-18
26. Luke 21:22
27. Matthew 24:19-20
28. Luke 21:23
29. Matthew 24:21
30. Mark 13:19
31. Luke 21:24
32. Mark 13:20
33. Matthew 24:23-24
34. Mark 13:22
35. Mark 13:23
36. Matthew 24:26
37. Matthew 24:27
38. Luke 17:25-27
39. Luke 17:28-33
40. Luke 17:34-36
41. Matthew 24:42
42. Matthew 24:36
43. Matthew 24:43-44
44. Luke 17:37
45. Matthew 24:29
46. Luke 21:25-26
47. Matthew 24:30-31
48. Mark 13:27
49. Luke 21:28
50. Matthew 24:32
51. Luke 21:29
52. Luke 21:31
53. Mark 13:29
54. Matthew 24:34-35
55. Matthew 25:31-34
56. Matthew 25:35-39
57. Matthew 25:40
58. Matthew 25:41-43
59. Matthew 25:44-46

26. KEEPING HIS WORDS

He that has my commands, and keeps them, is he that loves me: and he that loves me will be loved of my Father, and I will love him, and will reveal myself to him.[1] Yes, if a man loves me, he will keep my words: and my Father will love him, and we will come to him, and make our home with him.[2]

Those with an honest and good heart, having heard the word, keep it, and bring forth fruit with patience.[3] Yes, blessed are they that hear the word of God and keep it.[4] If you love me, keep my commandments.[5] And when you have done all those things which are commanded you, say, "We are unworthy servants: We have done that which is our duty to do."[6]

Whoever comes to me, and hears my sayings, and does them, I will show you who he is like: He is like a man which built a house, and digged deep and laid the foundation on a rock: and when the flood arose, the stream beat violently upon that house, and could not shake it: for it was founded upon a rock.[7]

My mother and brothers are those which hear the word of God, and do it.[8] If you keep my saying, you will never see death.[9] Yes, he that hears my word, and believes on him that sent me, has everlasting life, and will not come into condemnation, but is passed from death unto life.[10] If you know these things, happy are you if you do them.[11] Yes if you abide in me, and my words abide in you, you shall ask what you will, and it will be done unto you.[12] If you keep my commandments you will abide in my love.[13]

You are my friends, if you do whatever I command you.[14]

References:
1. John 14:21
2. John 14:23
3. Luke 8:15
4. Luke 11:28
5. John 14:15
6. Luke 17:10
7. Luke 6:47-48
8. Luke 8:21
9. John 8:51
10. John 5:24
11. John 13:17
12. John 15:7
13. John 15:10
14. John 15:14

27. REJECTING HIS WORDS

Why do you call me, Lord, Lord, and do not the things which I say?[1] Every one that hears these sayings of mine, and doesn't do them, shall be compared to a foolish man, which built his house upon the sand: And the rain fell, and the floods came, and the winds blew, and beat upon that house; and it fell: and great was the fall of it.[2]

He that does not love me, does not keep my sayings: and the word which you hear is not mine, but the Father's which sent me.[3] If any man hears my words and doesn't believe, I judge him not: for I came not to judge the world, but to save the world. He that rejects me, and doesn't receive my words, has one that judges him: the word that I have spoken, the same will judge him in the last day. For I have not spoken of myself; but the Father which sent me, he gave me a commandment, what I would say, and what I should speak.[4]

He that is of God, hears God's words: you therefore hear them not, because you are not of God.[5]

References:
1. Luke 6:46
2. Matthew 7:26-27
3. John 14:24
4. John 12:47-49
5. John 8:47

28. JESUS' FINAL INSTRUCTIONS

Thus it is written, and thus it behoved Christ to suffer, and to rise from the dead the third day: And that repentance and remission of sins should be preached in his name among all nations, beginning at Jerusalem. And you are witnesses of these things.[1] Peace be unto you: as my Father has sent me, even so send I you. **And when he had said this, he breathed on them, and said to them,** Receive the Holy Ghost: Whose sins you forgive, they are forgiven; If you retain the sins of any, they are retained.[2]

Behold, I send the promise of my Father upon you: but wait in the city of Jerusalem, until you have been clothed with power from on high.[3] All power is given unto me in heaven and in earth.[4] Go ye into all the world, and preach the gospel to every creature,[5] teaching all nations to observe all things I commanded you.[6] And he that believes and is baptized will be saved; but he that doesn't believe will be damned.[7] Baptize them in the name of the Father and of the Son, and of the Holy Ghost.[6]

And these signs will follow them that believe; In my name they will cast out devils; they will speak with new tongues; They will take up serpents; and if they drink any deadly thing, it will not hurt them; they will lay hands on the sick, and they will recover.[8]

And, lo, I am with you always, even unto the end of the world. Amen.[6]

References:
1. Luke 24:46-48
2. John 20:21-23
3. Luke 24:49
4. Matthew 28:18
5. Mark 16:15
6. Matthew 28:19-20
7. Mark 16:16
8. Mark 16:17-18

Other "Pure Word Products"
_____

THE BIBLE INCORPORATED - IN YOUR LIFE, JOB AND BUSINESS

A pocket-sized, leather bound compilation of over 2,000 scriptures arranged in conversation format into 101 work and business topics, giving you a decided advantage in the workforce or at home. 305 pages.

LOVE LIFTERS

Pocket-sized, 16 page compilations of scriptures, in greeting card format, when someone you love needs a lift.